23.33

W9-CNM-681

FEB 0 0 2007

## INDIAN TRAILS
## PUBLIC LIBRARY DISTRICT
### WHEELING, ILLINOIS  60090
**847-459-4100**

# Today's Superstars
## Entertainment

# Usher

PROPERTY OF NIAGARA FALLS
PUBLIC LIBRARY DISTRICT

by Geoffrey M. Horn

GARETHSTEVENS
GS
PUBLISHING
A Member of the WRC Media Family of Companies

Please visit our web site at: www.garethstevens.com
For a free color catalog describing Gareth Stevens Publishing's
list of high-quality books and multimedia programs, call
1-800-542-2595 (USA) or 1-800-387-3178 (Canada).
Gareth Stevens Publishing's fax: (414) 332-3567.

Library of Congress Cataloging-in-Publication Data

Horn, Geoffrey M.
    Usher / by Geoffrey M. Horn.
        p. cm. — (Today's superstars. Entertainment)
    Includes bibliographical references, discography, and index.
    ISBN 0-8368-4235-9 (lib. bdg.)
    1. Usher—Juvenile literature.   2. Rhythm and blues musicians—
United States—Biography—Juvenile literature.   I. Title.
ML3930.U84H67    2005
782.421643'092—dc22
    [B]                                        2005046502

This edition first published in 2006 by
**Gareth Stevens Publishing**
A Member of the WRC Media Family of Companies
330 West Olive Street, Suite 100
Milwaukee, WI  53212  USA

This edition copyright © 2006 by Gareth Stevens, Inc.

Editor:  Jim Mezzanotte
Art direction and design:  Tammy West
Picture research:  Diane Laska-Swanke

Photo credits:  Cover, © Kevin Mazur/WireImage.com; p. 5 © Michael
Caulfield/WireImage.com; p. 6 © Timothy A. Clary/AFP/Getty Images;
p. 9 © Kevin Kane/WireImage.com; p. 10 Photofest; p. 13 © Paul
Natkin/WireImage.com; p. 16 © John Shearer/WireImage.com; p. 20
© Paramount. Courtesy: Everett Collection, Inc.; p. 23 © Robin Platzer/
Twin Images/Getty Images; pp. 25, 26 © Frank Micelotta/Getty Images

All rights reserved.  No part of this book may be reproduced, stored in a retrieval
system, or transmitted in any form or by any means, electronic, mechanical,
photocopying, recording, or otherwise, without the prior written permission
of the copyright holder.

Printed in the United States of America

1 2 3 4 5 6 7 8 9 08 07 06 05

# Contents

Chapter 1 Showman.....................4

Chapter 2 Big Time.....................8

Chapter 3 Growing Up Fast ...........14

Chapter 4 His Way ....................19

Chapter 5 Confessions ................24

Time Line .............................29

Glossary .............................30

To Find Out More .....................31

Index ................................32

# Chapter 1  Showman

Sunday evening, February 13, 2005, is a sweet night for Usher. He's at the annual Grammy Awards ceremony. Usher is up for eight Grammy Awards, and he wins three. But the awards are not the only reason the night has so much meaning for him.

Queen Latifah does the intro for his big Grammy number. "You take some of the sleekness of Sam Cooke," she begins. "Some of that deep soul of James Brown. And some of the funky street smarts of Prince." Put them all together, she says, and "you got one hell of a man.... It's time to get caught up with the man — Usher!"

Caught up — that's the cue for Usher to sing his hit "Caught Up," from the smash album *Confessions*. We hear the boom of drums and bass, followed by background chanting and a hint of synth. Usher appears bathed in fog and blue lights. He dances from stage to stage. He leaps. He kicks and struts. He does a split, then a back flip.

Offstage, Usher doesn't look big — he's only 5 feet, 9 inches (1.8 meters) tall. But on the Grammy stage tonight, in his crisp dark suit and hat, he's the biggest man around.

Fans got "caught up" in Usher's dazzling performance at the 2005 Grammy Awards.

## Godfather of Hip-Hop?

James Brown has never been shy about his place in music history. In 2003, he told a reporter, "Disco is James Brown. Hip-hop is James Brown. Rap is James Brown." A lot of hip-hop artists would agree with him. Chuck D of Public Enemy once said, "To this day, there has been no one near as funky." Many hip-hop records use samples from "Funky Drummer" and other James Brown classics.

The Grammy Awards show got a double dose of soul and R&B when James Brown and Usher shared the stage.

Or maybe not. When "Caught Up" ends, the band takes up a funky beat. Standing on the other side of the stage is James Brown. He's been called Mr. Dynamite, Soul Brother Number One, and the Hardest Working Man in Show Business. These days, he's known as the Godfather of Soul. He's been in the Rock and Roll Fall of Fame since its beginning.

Tonight, he is is dressed to kill, in a flashy red suit. He's singing one of his most famous numbers, "Get Up … Sex Machine."

If this is a challenge, Usher is up to it. He matches Brown note for note, line for line, step for step. The crowd loves it. Finally, the two men hug each other. The Godfather of Soul calls the kid from Atlanta "the new Godson."

From the Godfather to the Godson. From "Get Up" to "Caught Up." In the world of soul and R&B, a torch has been passed.

## Fact File

Sam Cooke was one of the first soul singers. His hits in the 1950s and 1960s included "You Send Me," "Twistin' the Night Away," and "Shake."

# Chapter 2

# Big Time

Usher Raymond IV was born in Dallas, Texas, on October 14, 1978. On the VH1 show *Driven*, his grandfather explained how Usher got his nickname, Big Time. His grandfather said Usher "just had kind of a special glow about himself."

Usher's father, Usher Raymond III, played little part in his life. He was "into drugs, into havin' a great time, and that was it," Usher's mother, Jonnetta Patton, told VH1. She said he was abusive. "He loved me, in his own way," she said, "and he actually loved his kid. But he just wasn't right for us." In 1980, Jonnetta left Usher's dad. She and Usher moved to Chattanooga, Tennessee. They lived

## Fact File

Chattanooga is located in southeast Tennessee, near the border with Georgia. The city has a rich musical history. The great blues singer Bessie Smith was born in Chattanooga more than a century ago.

## What Does the "IV" Mean?

The "IV" in Usher's name means "the fourth." The "III" in his father's name means "the third." Roman numerals such as "III" and "IV" based on a number system created in ancient Rome more than two thousand years ago. Roman numerals are used in more than just names. The thirty-ninth pro football championship, played in 2005, was called Super Bowl XXXIX. In Roman numerals, the year 2005 is written MMV.

Usher with his mother, Jonnetta Patton.

Usher learned a great deal from the artists he grew up imitating. He still loves the music of Prince, Marvin Gaye, Michael Jackson, Stevie Wonder, and Donny Hathaway. "With everything that I've done, I make an effort to recognize where I came from," he told a reporter in 2004. "Those are the people who are very influential in helping me build who I am as an artist."

Usher took his stage show to Bryant Park, in New York City, for a 2004 appearance on *Good Morning America*.

in a mostly black neighborhood. Jonnetta
worked two jobs, so Usher spent much of
the next six years with his grandmother.

Music was a big part of family life when
Usher was growing up. As a boy, he would
imitate the records he heard. Stevie Wonder,
Marvin Gaye, and the Temptations were the
family favorites. Jonnetta was music director
of Saint Elmo's Missionary Church Choir.
By the time Usher was nine years old, he had
joined the choir. Soon, he was singing solos
in church.

## "I'm Gonna Be Rich Someday"

Usher was not a good student. "He was
rambunctious," one teacher recalled. "He
would rather play than read. He'd rather
play than write. He'd rather sing than do
any of it." Usher would tell her, "I'm gonna
be rich someday. And everybody's
gonna know my name."

In middle school, Usher
discovered girls. He was always
singing to them, talking with
them, trying to kiss them.

## Fact File

Many artists have had hit
songs on the Motown label.
Stevie Wonder, Marvin Gaye, the
Temptations, and Michael Jackson
all scored huge hits for Motown.

Usher's teachers had a tough time keeping him under control.

When Usher was twelve years old, he joined a boy band in Chattanooga called Nu Beginning. The boys were managed by a man named Darryl Wheeler. He taught them how to sing, dance, and move as a group on stage. The boys became close friends. "Usher is not a superstar to me," Wheeler told a reporter. "He's still the boy that lived in my house and slept in the same room with my son and ate at my table."

Usher was happy with the group, but his mother was not. She wanted her son to be a solo star. She forced Usher to leave Nu Beginning. "You're so much bigger than that," she told her son. "You could stand alone."

## Fact File

Darryl Wheeler has put out a DVD called *When Dreams Are Shattered*. The video tells his side of the Nu Beginning story. These days, Usher and his mother have little to say about Wheeler and Nu Beginning.

## Beginnings and Endings

Darryl Wheeler and the members of Nu Beginning feel Usher has never given them enough credit. One group member, Anthony Byrd, described a difficult moment in 1998. Usher was in Chattanooga to sing at Bessie Smith Hall. After the show, as Usher was about to ride away in his limo, he saw Byrd and Wheeler. But he didn't speak with them.

"That was a real crushing moment for Darryl and me," Byrd told the *Chattanooga Times Free Press* in 2004. "Here was the man that clothed him and fed him, and he wouldn't even roll the window down and shake his hand."

Usher made his first records with Nu Beginning. A CD containing his tracks with the group came out in 2002.

By 1998, Usher was a solo star, and he saw little of his former friends in Nu Beginning.

# Chapter 3

# Growing Up Fast

When Usher was thirteen years old, his mother took him out of Nu Beginning. She and Usher then moved to Atlanta, Georgia. Atlanta was a much larger city than Chattanooga. It was a rising power in the music business.

In Atlanta, Usher's mother pushed him to show off his solo talents. Usher began performing at talent shows in the city. At one show, he was spotted by A. J. Alexander. Alexander had ties with some of the major players on the Atlanta music scene. He was sure Usher could be a big star, and he began working with him.

Alexander knew Bryant Reid, of LaFace Records. He invited Bryant to come see Usher perform at a talent contest. Bryant was blown away. "This little kid came on stage and was absolutely phenomenal," he recalled. "All of the girls in the audience were screaming like crazy."

Bryant wasted no time. He called his brother, Antonio "L.A." Reid, who was the head of LaFace Records. A day later, Usher sang for L.A.

"When Usher came to my office," L.A. said later, "I called in all of the women on my staff to hear him. And I watched this kid just charm them. I knew right then he had it." He offered Usher a record deal on the spot.

## Roadblocks

The Reid brothers thought Usher was on the fast track to stardom. But as Usher neared his fifteenth birthday, his career began running into roadblocks. His first single for LaFace Records, "Call Me a Mack," appeared on the soundtrack for the 1993 film *Poetic Justice*. The movie starred Janet Jackson and Tupac Shakur. It was a modest hit. But Usher's cut had a hard time breaking through.

Then his voice began to change from a boy's into a man's. Usher worked

## Fact File

When Usher was fourteen, he appeared on national TV for the first time. He was a winner on *Star Search*, hosted by Ed McMahon.

## Teen Wonders

Many pop stars have made it big while still in their teens. Frankie Lymon was only thirteen when he had a number-one R&B hit in 1956 with "Why Do Fools Fall in Love?" Brenda Lee was fifteen when she first topped the pop charts with "I'm Sorry" in 1960. Stevie Wonder was twelve when "Fingertips (Part 2)" became a chart-topper in 1963 for the Motown label. (He was called Little Stevie Wonder back then.) When the Jackson Five scored big with "I Want You Back" in 1970, their lead singer was only eleven. His name? Michael Jackson.

Stevie Wonder has had a long and very successful career. But many other young pop stars have had problems later in life. Frankie Lymon became a drug addict, for example, and he died at the age of twenty-five. In the 1980s, Michael Jackson became a pop superstar. But since then, he has led a troubled life.

**Antonio "L.A." Reid joins Usher at the *Soul Train* Music Awards in 2005. The pop superstar received a special award as Entertainer of the Year.**

with a coach to help him find his new voice and learn how to control it. At this point, however, the record company wasn't sure what to do with the kid.

L.A. Reid thought he had the answer. He got in touch with a hot young producer, Sean "Puffy" Combs. By 1994, Puffy had his own label, Bad Boy. He offered to take Usher to New York City and work with him.

Usher lived and worked with Combs for a year. Puffy and his posse were living the rock & roll lifestyle. Parties, women, drugs, and cash — Usher saw it all. His mother, meanwhile, was getting nervous. She called Combs often, sometimes three or four times a day. Combs told her everything was fine. "To be honest," Puffy told VH1, "sometimes we bent the truth a little bit."

Reid and Combs wanted to change Usher's image. He was fifteen years old, a girl-crazy kid from down south. They wanted to turn him into a street-smart bad boy from the big city. Did it work? Not really. Usher's 1994 album with Puffy, *Usher*, didn't do well.

## Fact File

L.A. Reid and Kenneth "Babyface" Edmonds have worked together as writers, performers, and producers. They started LaFace Records in Atlanta in 1989. The company name includes a part of each man's nickname.

LaFace Records tried a lot of tricks to sell the album. *Billboard* magazine reported that the company put a hundred thousand coupons in packages of Teen Image deodorant. The coupons could be exchanged at Musicland stores for cassettes of Usher's songs. Each cassette came with a discount coupon for the full-length album.

Thousands of postcards were sent to record stores and radio stations. LaFace also paid for big ads in magazines such as *Seventeen*, *Sassy*, and *Teen*. Company people took to the streets. They put flyers and stickers in skating rinks, dance clubs, and other teen hangouts. They worked as hard as they could to turn *Usher* into a megahit. It didn't happen.

The songs didn't really suit Usher. The attitude didn't, either. "The whole bad boy thing, me frowning for the camera — that wasn't me," he later admitted.

## Fact File

Sean "Puffy" Combs has also used the names Puff Daddy and, later, P. Diddy. He won a Grammy for Best Rap Album in 1997 with *No Way Out*. Combs has worked with Mary J. Blige, Mariah Carey, Notorious B.I.G., and many other artists.

# His Way

# Chapter 4

After his first album flopped, LaFace Records thought about dropping Usher. But the teenage singer was not about to give up. Although his records didn't sell well, his stage shows got better and better. Girls loved it when he sang directly to them, and they screamed when he took off his shirt on stage.

The record company agreed to give him another shot. For his second LaFace album, Usher was teamed with Jermaine Dupri. Unlike Puffy Combs, Dupri was a native of Atlanta and was based there.

For about six months, Usher lived and worked with Jermaine. They went to clubs together, searching for the hottest sounds and fashions. Jermaine even listened in on Usher's phone calls. He wanted to

## Fact File

Of the videos he's made so far, Usher says "U Remind Me" is his favorite.

As a singer and dancer, Usher is often compared to Michael Jackson. In 2004, Usher was asked whether he was the new King of Pop. "If I was given that title, I would accept it," he answered. "And I would hope that I would represent it properly, because Michael Jackson held it down for almost forty years."

Usher's producer, Jermaine Dupri, is linked to another famous Jackson — Michael's sister Janet. In recent years, Jermaine has become both her partner and her producer.

Brandy and Usher in the TV comedy *Moesha*.

hear how Usher actually talked to girls. He then wrote songs for Usher based on the way the younger man really spoke.

Dupri understood that Usher had grown up with old-school R&B. He gave the singer a softer sound, smooth and sexy, with a more flowing vocal line. The work paid off. Usher's 1997 album, *My Way*, went on to sell more than six million copies in the United States alone. "You Make Me Wanna" and "Nice & Slow" took Usher to the top of the singles charts. *Billboard* magazine chose him as Artist of the Year for 1998.

## The Big Picture

Usher worked hard to build on the success of *My Way*. "Ever since I became a singer, I went after the entertainment part of it," he said in 1998. "Entertainment doesn't consist of just music. There's also performance and total dedication to your work."

In the late 1990s, Usher appeared several times on the TV comedy *Moesha*. He played one of Moesha's boyfriends on the show, which starred the singer Brandy.

## Fact File

*Billboard* named Usher Artist of the Year for a second time in 2004, the year *Confessions* came out.

He also had an acting role on a daytime TV soap opera, *The Bold and the Beautiful*.

Movies were part of Usher's game plan, too. In 1998, he appeared on the big screen in a horror flick, *The Faculty*. He had a bigger role in the 1999 drama *Light It Up*. Usher has had other film roles since then. But no one is begging him to give up his day job as a singer.

After releasing a live album in 1999, Usher went back into the recording studio. He began laying down tracks for a new album. It was supposed to be called *All About U*. But the project went sour. Fearing disaster, L.A. Reid shut it down.

Usher had to go back into the studio and start again. This time, the outcome was much better. The album was called *8701*. Released on Arista Records, it sold more than eight million copies worldwide. Two singles from *8701*, "U Remind Me" and "U Got It Bad," each hit the top spot on the pop and R&B charts. The two singles also won Usher his first two Grammy Awards.

## Fact File

The title *8701* comes from the date the album was released: August 7, 2001, or 8-7-01.

greatest pop singer ever. "My Way" became one of his greatest hits. Giving Usher's album the same name as a Sinatra classic was a gutsy move. The choice of the title showed just how big a star the record company thought Usher could be.

Along with Usher, the young cast of *The Faculty* included (from left to right) Jordana Brewster, Shawn Hatosy, Clea DuVall, Josh Hartnett, and Elijah Wood.

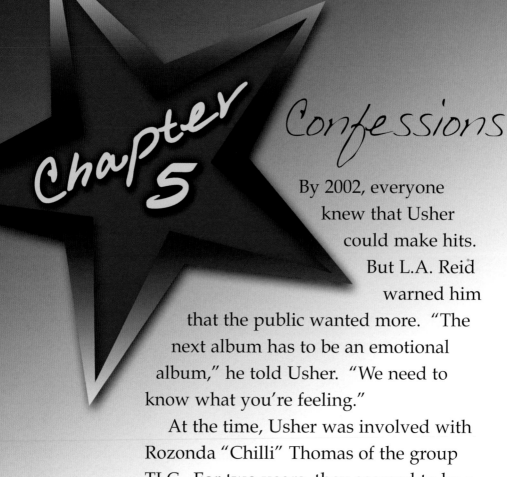

# Chapter 5

# Confessions

By 2002, everyone
knew that Usher
could make hits.
But L.A. Reid
warned him
that the public wanted more. "The
next album has to be an emotional
album," he told Usher. "We need to
know what you're feeling."

At the time, Usher was involved with
Rozonda "Chilli" Thomas of the group
TLC. For two years, they seemed to be a
very loving couple. She called him "Papa
Bear." He called her "Lil' Big Mama."

In 2004, they broke up. It wasn't pretty.
Chilli went on radio in February and said,
"Usher did the ultimate no-no to me, and
I will never be with him ever again."

Usher's new album, *Confessions*, came
out in March. It had some powerhouse
cuts, including the megahit "Yeah!"
with Ludacris and crunk shouter Lil Jon.

But the gossip focused on a quieter song, "Confessions, Part 2."

In the song, Usher admits he has " a chick on the side" who says "she's got one on the way." Was it true? Had he really cheated on Chilli? If so, was the other woman having his baby?

The answer to the first question seems clear. When asked by *Ebony* magazine, Usher admitted he had been unfaithful. He also said he had confessed to Chilli.

Usher signs copies of *Confessions* at a record store in New York City.

## Hot, Hot, Hot

In 2004, Usher made history when he had three top-10 singles on the pop charts at the same time. The Beatles had three singles in the top ten in 1964. So did the Bee Gees in 1978, when the disco craze of *Saturday Night Fever* was at its peak.

Usher's three chart-topping songs were "Burn," "Confessions, Part 2," and "Yeah!" All came from the *Confessions* album. He had another number-one single in late 2004: "My Boo," with Alicia Keys. On the *Billboard* magazine Hot 100 singles chart for the whole year, "Yeah!" and "Burn" ranked first and second. The last artists to own the two top spots on the year-end Hot 100 were the Beatles in 1964, with "I Want to Hold Your Hand" and "She Loves You."

**A Showtime cable special caught Usher on a steamy night in Puerto Rico.**

"I told her the truth. Most men wouldn't do it. Most women wouldn't do it. I'm a man. I can own up to what I did. I ain't trying to hide from it. I ain't perfect."

Was there a baby? "I didn't get a woman pregnant when I was dating Chilli," Usher told *Ebony*.

Maybe the details in the song are true. Or maybe they're not. What's most important is that the feeling is real, and the singing is some of the best he's ever done.

## Taking Care of Business

Usher was the top-selling recording artist of 2004. No one else even came close. A year after *Confessions* first hit the charts, it had sold eight million copies in the United States, and the album was still going strong.

How far can Usher go? He's interested in fashion. He's working on a couple of movie projects. He's starting his own label, Usher Records. He owns a piece of a pro basketball team. Yet he's still in his twenties.

Usher isn't the only pop star to put his money in NBA

## Fact File

TLC's hit singles in the 1990s included "Creep," "Waterfalls," "No Scrubs," and "Unpretty."

27

basketball. Jay-Z is part owner of the New Jersey Nets. Nelly is co-owner of the Charlotte Bobcats. But Usher may have the sweetest deal of all. He invested in the Cleveland Cavaliers. So Usher owns a piece of one of the hottest names in pro basketball: LeBron James.

Usher's imagination runs wild when he talks about business deals. He'd like to market his own brands of clothing, watches, and perfume. He also told *Essence* magazine that he might come out with a line of facial and acne products. How about an album of his own music? "Sometime in the future," he said. But not for a couple of years.

In March 2005, Usher gave his fans a taste of where he wants to take them. At the end of a special on the Showtime cable channel, he said, "I don't do drugs.... I'm addicted to music. But I'm a businessman before I'm a musician."

"We're going to make history," he concluded. "We're going to turn it up a notch, I promise you."

## Fact File

Usher made more than $25 million from concert ticket and CD sales in 2004.

# Time Line

| | |
|---|---|
| **1978** | Usher Raymond IV is born October 14 in Dallas, Texas. |
| **1992** | Wins on *Star Search* and signs with LaFace Records. |
| **1994** | His first album, *Usher*, flops. |
| **1997** | Has his first top R&B album, *My Way*, and first top single, "You Make Me Wanna." Begins appearing on the TV show *Moesha*. |
| **1999** | Appears in the film *Light it up*. |
| **2001** | *8701* is released. |
| **2004** | *Confessions* becomes the year's top-selling album. |
| **2005** | Usher wins three Grammy Awards and stars in his own Showtime cable TV special. |

# Glossary

**abusive** — causing physical or mental harm.

**charts** — in the music business, lists of the most popular, best-selling artists.

**crunk** — a kind of hip-hop party music. The word is usually described as a mixture of "crazy" and "drunk."

**Grammy** — award given by the recording industry to musicians and other people working in music.

**imitate** — sound, look, or act like someone else.

**phenomenal** — outstanding.

**producers** — the people responsible for the overall sound of recordings.

**rambunctious** — wild or out of control.

**R&B** — short for rhythm and blues. At first, R&B was a mix of blues and dance rhythms. Today, it includes many kinds of African American pop music.

**samples** — in music, bits of previously recorded music that are used in new songs.

**solos** — in a piece of music, parts performed by a single voice or instrument.

**soul** — in music, a mix of R&B and gospel, a form of Christian religious music. Soul first became popular in the 1950s.

# To Find Out More

**Books**

*The History of Motown.* African American Achievers (series). Virginia Aronson (Chelsea House)

*Usher.* Blue Banner Biographies (series). John Torres (Mitchell Lane)

*Usher.* Star Files (series). Dan Whitcombe (Raintree)

*Working in Music and Dance.* My Future Career (series). Margaret McAlpine (Gareth Stevens)

**Videos**

*Usher: Live-Evolution 8701* (Red Distribution) NR

**Web Sites**

Rollingstone.com: Usher
*www.rollingstone.com/artist/_/id/1244/usher*
News about Usher from *Rolling Stone* magazine

UsherWorld
*www.usherworld.com*
Usher's official web site, with news, tour dates, fan club links, and other information

VH1.com: Usher
*www.vh1.com/artists/az/id_1270/artist.jhtml*
Usher news from the video music channel

# Index

*8701* 22
Alexander, A. J. 14
Atlanta, Georgia 14, 19
*Billboard* magazine 18, 21, 26
Brown, James 4, 6, 7
"Burn" 26
"Call Me a Mack" 15
"Caught Up" 4, 7
Chattanooga, Tennessee 8, 12, 14
Combs, Sean "Puffy" 17, 18, 19
*Confessions* 4, 21, 24, 25, 27
"Confessions, Part 2" 25, 26, 27
Cooke, Sam 4, 7
Dupri, Jermaine 19, 20, 21
*Faculty, The* 22, 23

Gaye, Marvin 10, 11
Grammy Awards 4, 5, 6, 18, 22
Jackson, Janet 15, 20
Jackson, Michael 10, 11, 16, 20
James, LeBron 28
Keys, Alicia 26
LaFace Records 14, 15, 17, 18, 19
*Light It Up* 22
*Moesha* 20, 21
Motown 11, 16
"My Boo" 26
*My Way* 21, 23
"Nice & Slow" 21
Nu Beginning 12, 13, 14
Patton, Jonnetta 8, 9, 11, 12, 14, 17
Prince 4, 10
Queen Latifah 4

Raymond, Usher, III 8
Reid, Antonio "L.A." 15, 16, 17, 22, 24
Reid, Bryant 14
Sinatra, Frank 23
Smith, Bessie 8
*Star Search* 15
Temptations 11
Thomas, Rozonda "Chilli" 24, 25, 27
TLC 24, 27
"U Got It Bad" 22
"U Remind Me" 19, 22
*Usher* 17, 18
Wheeler, Darryl 12, 13
Wonder, Stevie 10, 11, 16
"Yeah!" 24, 26
"You Make Me Wanna" 21

## About the Author

Geoffrey M. Horn has been a fan of music, movies, and sports for as long as he can remember. He has written more than a dozen books for young people and adults, along with hundreds of articles on many different subjects. He lives in southwestern Virginia, in the foothills of the Blue Ridge Mountains, with his wife, their collie, and four cats. He dedicates this book to C.B., L.H., J.L., E.G., M.B., M.E., and the other girls from way back when.

3 1125 00629 1338